MOUNTBATTEN IN RETROSPECT

MOUNTBATTEN
in Retrospect

ALAN CAMPBELL-JOHNSON
CIE, OBE, Hon. D.Litt.

SPANTECH & LANCER

Three appreciations, first published as an anthology 1997

© Alan Campbell-Johnson 1997

ISBN 1 897829 32 9

Published by
Spantech & Lancer
Spantech House
Lagham Road
South Godstone
Surrey RH9 8HB, England
Fax (1342) 892584

Spantech USA
3986 Ernst Road
Hartford, Wi 53027, USA
Fax (414) 6739064

Spantech & Lancer
119 Stratton Cres. S.W.
Calgary, Alberta
Canada T3H 1T7

Lancer Publishers & Distributors
56 Gautam Nagar
New Delhi 110 049, India
Fax (11) 6862077

Printed at
Sona Printers, New Delhi

British Library Cataloguing-in-Publication Data.
A catalogue record for this book is available
from the British Library

Contents

Preface

THE ADDRESS which I gave to the Royal Institute of
International Affairs in November 1948 within six
months of my return from service as Press Attache to
Lord Mountbatten, the last Viceroy and first
constitutional Governor of independent India, has
continued to provide me ever since with what I described
at the time as being 'a natural final entry to sum up and
round off my daily record'. I was referring to the daily
notes I had kept during Lord Mountbatten's term of
office and which were to be later published as *Mission
With Mountbatten* (1951). I have not deliberately sought
over the ensuing years to indulge in hindsight or to
point a moral and adorn a tale. Having survived to see
the celebration of the fiftieth anniversary of transfer of
power to India and Pakistan, I have felt constrained to
stay in the present tense the youthful and privileged
eye-witness reporter of history in the making.

There have however been just three special occasions
spread over wide intervals during the ensuing half-
century when I was called upon to take serious account
of the passage of time and the unfolding of historical
perceptions and to see Mountbatten in retrospect.

My first formal return to the subject was an address
to the East India Association in March 1952 given to
an audience which included an impressive array of
former Indian Civil Service officials capable of submitting
my thesis to most searching scrutiny, and representing

at a high and authoritative level the British point of view. I was privileged and relieved to have as my Chairman on that occasion Lord Listowel, the last British Secretary of State for India, whose cogent and supportive comments helped to narrow the credibility gap created by my seeking to give a lecture to such a glittering assembly on such a subject.

Thirty-three years were to pass before a further opportunity arose in 1985 to return to the theme. I was a whole generation from the subject by now. Mountbatten had been assassinated six years previously and had just become the subject of an official biography—a project which he had refused to authorise in his life-time.

Philip Ziegler's masterly study provided the platform for a fresh appraisal of Mountbatten's entire public record, and the Editor of the *Encounter* invited me to produce a personal commentary within the context of Ziegler's researches and my own six years experience as a member of the headquarters staff of Mountbatten as Chief of Combined Operations, Supreme Allied Commander South-East Asia and Viceroy. They were to some extent linked, as Ziegler specifically refers, to the various taped interviews which I had with Mountbatten over the years and which were compiled to provide source material for a putative official biography. In my *Encounter* article I do my best to take account an emerging critical and cold climate of opinion which serves to affect all historical judgements of the past—a deeper view of developments that could or could not be foreseen or controlled, the balance of risk and the emphasis on limiting factors. Ziegler, exasperated by Mountbatten's egocentric tendency to translate his record into the populist terms of television and audio-visual dialect generally, was to open the floodgates to a host of polemical and often vituperative critics who in the ensuing years sought with gusto to diminish and demean Mountbatten's whole career, capacity and integrity. Ziegler however—almost in spite of himself—remained convinced that he had been dealing with a great man but the destructive process was over the next decade to be exploited to extreme lengths by others less qualified than him, to pass judgement.

It was indeed a reductio ad absurdum, and I was to have the opportunity in April 1996 under the auspices of a seminar at Southampton University to return for a third and final assessment. Although this particular 'Pilgrims's Progress' takes me beyond the physical confines of the Indian transfer of power, I come to the broad conclusion that Mountbatten's terms of service as Chief of Combined Operations and Supreme Allied Commander were effectively apprenticeships for his role as Viceroy, and that historically it was essentially the same assignment carried out in three distinct phases or forms and all were concerned with the techniques of handling strategic transfers of power. By bringing together the texts of my 1952, 1985 and 1996 commentaries I hope to have provided a relevant and appropriate supplement to the anniversary edition of *Mission With Mountbatten*.

Westminster   ALAN CAMPBELL-JOHNSON
March 1997

Reflections on the Transfer of Power

Lord Listowel, Chairman, introduced Mr Campbell-Johnson:

Our speaker was one of the talented members of the small personal staff which Lord Mountbatten took with him to New Delhi. As Press Attache to the Viceroy it was his job to interpret policy to the Indian, Commonwealth and foreign press, at a time when public opinion, all over the world, was following daily events with breathless interest. He seems to have known everyone, and seen everything. The high opinion in which he was held by Lord Mountbatten himself was never more conspicuous than when he was sent on a political mission to Hyderabad, at a moment when it was hoped the Nizam might accede to the new dominion. Of his book I will only say this. When I was a history student at Balliol, the first thing my tutor told me was that sources mattered much more than history. Those who love reading history will find Mr Campbell-Johnson's diary an original source of information, and a reliable one, about an episode which will no doubt come to be regarded, like the Russian Revolution, or the rise of the Nazi Party in Germany, as one of the turning points in the history of the twentieth century. This book holds one's attention, not only as an accurate description of epoch-making events, but as a highly intelligent commentary on people and policies.

When I first went to the India Office in 1944, my chief, Mr Leo Amery, asked me somewhat nervously whether a message I had just sent to Pandit Nehru in the gaol where he was imprisoned had reflected upon the policy of the Government of India. He was relieved, I think, when I told him that it had been merely an expression of my high personal regard. When I left the India office in 1947, Pandit Nehru was the first Prime Minister of the new Dominion of India. Such was the measure of the political metamorphosis which had taken place in those years, assuming its final shape in the few months of Lord Mountbatten's viceroyalty.

This period of the transfer of power is still sufficiently close to be a subject of lively controversy. But it would be a fatal mistake to suppose that continuing British rule in India might have been a viable alternative to transfer of power. We had been warned by Lord Wavell that the administration of British India was running down, and that in an exceedingly short time we should no longer be able to control it.

This indeed was a corollary of the decision, early in the war, to cease recruitment to the Indian Civil Service and the Indian Police. The substitution of a military government, supported by an Army of Occupation, for the civilian administration of British India was not a course of action which any government at home could seriously consider. The possibility of an alternate policy to the transfer of power should, therefore, be dismissed from our minds. The scope of controversy is in this way narrowed down to the manner and method by which the two legatees came into their inheritance. Here, of course, there is room for honest differences of opinion. If I may give you the opinion held by the British Government at the time, I would say that Lord Mountbatten's achievement, in face of the many baffling difficulties which confronted him, far exceeded our most optimistic expectations.

You will remember that when he went out to India, Congess had already declared itself in favour of India becoming a Sovereign Republic outside the Commonwealth. It was surely an extraordinary feat of statesmanship to persuade the Indian leaders, in a few weeks, that, in spite of their unhappy memories, the independence they prized for their people would find its fulfilment within the familiar framework of the British Commonwealth. But probably the most lasting benefit, alike to the Commonwealth and the outside world, which derives directly from the Mountbatten viceroyalty and governor-generalship, was the dispersal of that cloud of bitterness and suspicion which had for so long obscured our relations with the subcontinent. Old resentments were replaced, almost overnight, by a warmth of affection and regard for Britain and the British which still sustains a volume of goodwill unparalleled in the past.

Mr Alan Campbell-Johnson's presentation:

May I say at the outset that I regard it a signal privilege to have been invited to address the East India Association on the great theme of the transfer of power to India and Pakistan. I felt particularly honoured that the Chairman should be Lord Listowel who, as the last Secretary of State for India, invested that high office with such dignity and distinction during those momentous days of decision. I deeply appreciate his kind remarks about my own modest role at the time, but nothing that he has said can remove from me a personal sense of inadequacy in standing before the members of this Association so many of whom have given long and devoted service in India and helped to uphold in their own careers the highest traditions of the Indian Civil Service.

Lord Listowel has been good enough to mention to you the diary record I maintained, and published, of my experiences on Lord Mountbatten's staff throughout his fifteen month term of office as the last Viceroy and first constitutional Governor-General of the Dominion of India. For all its limitations, of which I am only too well aware, the book places me I believe in the category of the historian's favourite child—or should I say *enfant terrible?*—a primary source. It is at this point that I would like to follow the eminent example of Dr Conant, the President of Harvard, who in a remarkable address on Anglo-American relations in the atomic age started off by quoting the need for a lecturer to declare at the outset the nature of his bias. For purely objective history I suppose is just about as abortive a concept as

Goethe's Homunculus—the brain in the test tube, the mental process without the bodily substance.

Lord Mountbatten's Staff

Some critics in their comments have failed perhaps to appreciate my close proximity with the events described in my log book. Because it is largely taken up with Lord Mountbatten's view-point and with a steady commendation of his policy and actions I have been described as the uncritical hero-worshipper and a 'Mountbatten man'. Certainly I was a 'Mountbatten man' in the sense that my bias was that I agreed with what he was doing and how he was doing it. If I had not done so I think it may be safely assumed that I would not have stayed on. The essence of the matter was that Mountbatten was surrounded by a group of men—his regular ICS Secretariat together with his special task force headed by Lord Ismay. From the moment we combined forces in Delhi we worked together as a team. Individually they represented widely varying experience and outlook, but together not only were they the most talented body it has ever been my good fortune to work with, but their efforts were invested by a sense of union and urgency which it was an exhilarating experience to share. If we were Mountbatten's 'yes men' it was rather in the sense that we were wholly united in our resolve to secure an affirmative answer, and to approach the problem much in the mood of Mr Churchill's famous directive to Lord Mountbatten on an earlier occasion when he instructed him to pursue the project of Mulberry—'Pray', wrote the Prime

Minister, 'do not argue the difficulties, the difficulties will argue for themselves'.

It is not my intention that my comments today, four years later, should be in any sense an apologia for what I wrote then, but I have detected in a few of the comments aroused by my book what I regard as a basic misunderstanding of the policy and method Lord Mountbatten pursued. Because he succeeded in securing the agreement of the leaders quickly, it is assumed that he rushed the Indian leaders off their feet, getting them to sign along a dotted line without understanding what they were doing. The opposite was the truth. I doubt whether any draft agreement was thrashed out with such exhaustive line by line, and paragraph by paragraph discussion at such a high political level as the 3 June Plan. It was the reverse of an award.

A Unique Political Act

But regardless of the injection of a time limit the only prospect of settlement lay in securing it quickly, while the area of possible agreement had in effect been narrowed down to partition and a particular form of partition at that. Much is made of pointing a dramatic contrast between the years and months taken over administrative and legal partitions of far less pith and moment and the 72 days between Lord Mountbatten's arrival and 3 June announcement and the further 73 days to Independence itself. But it is just because a voluntary political transfer of power by partition was a unique and unconditional political act that such analogies cannot be drawn. It was a leap across a precipice, and, as has been justly observed, you cannot perform that particular feat in two or more jumps. Moreover, the Mountbatten plan was not simply the bringing forward of a time limit, the hastening of a political process. It in fact allowed for an administrative partition afterwards which was not subjected to any such guillotine and which was sheltered by a prior agreement on the major political issues in dispute. The argument that this political solution brought in its train grave and immediate civil discords should not be allowed to distract attention from the essential wisdom and effectiveness of this juxtaposition of political and administrative transfer. Indeed the operations of the various committees set up, such as the Partition Committee and the Joint Defence Council, went on uninterruptedly with what can only be regarded as astonishing smoothness, precision and goodwill.

A Settlement of the Highest Urgency

Four and a half years after the event I remain convinced of the profound wisdom of Mr Rajagopalachari's remark to Lord Mountbatten made during our visit to Calcutta early in 1948, 'If you had not transferred power when you did,' he said, 'there would have been no power to transfer', and what would have been the administrative consequences then? Moreover whether they were right or wrong, on one thing all the leaders were agreed, that the political settlement was of the highest urgency and that no administrative issue should be allowed to stand in the way of it. It may be argued that the leaders— their lives had been given up to the arts of political agitation—had no proper awareness of the implications of their demands, but I am convinced that nothing would have brought home to them the administrative facts of life short of the earliest possible acceptance of political responsibility. It was not therefore unawareness of the risks that prompted Lord Mountbatten and his staff to press forward, but rather the sense that we were dealing with a situation in which administrative safeguards could not predetermine independence but could only be the fruits of self-government.

'Tripatite Communal Madness'

While therefore this was the major premise of Lord Mountbatten's policy, in which I may say he was the interpreter of the British Government and fully supported by it, the vital question arises as to whether it took into account the special hazards induced by the communal tension, and whether the perilous situation in the Punjab and its tragic outcome were given due weight in the making of the larger decisions. Naturally the wounds have gone so deep, the weight of human suffering and the sense of political injustice is so great that it is difficult even to discuss this issue without summoning up the most violent emotional reactions.

In terms of the military risk I very much doubt whether any more preparation could have been laid even if more time had been allowed. The Punjab Boundary Force brought together in the areas most acutely affected, was probably the largest military concentration ever made in one place in time of peace.

Moreover, it was the response to a careful estimate of what would be required to prevent a civil war and it included armoured formations, artillery and air support. The provision of such a force was remarkable when it is kept in mind that it had to be summoned against the background of the leaders' insistence upon the immediate reconstitution and partitioning of the army and the need for a state of alert in other areas far distant from the Punjab storm centre—in particular Bengal and Calcutta. The truth is that in an atmosphere of tripartite communal madness the orthodox military sanction was virtually irrelevant. An army is not designed to save a population from self-slaughter.

If, therefore, the remedy was primarily political, how was the political responsibility discharged. Here again under the conditions prevailing I cannot see that anything other than a rapid transfer of power could have got the Punjab, in spite of the unstinting efforts of its brilliant governor, out of the operation of Section 93 government—government by decree. How such a government could have been maintained in face of the ever growing resistance of all three communities both to it and to themselves without jeopardizing the wider settlement, I do not know.

If Lord Mountbatten had allowed the Muslim League to form a ministry, it cannot be doubted in the light of later experience that disturbances would have broken out which might well have prejudiced the entire transfer of power. Lord Mountbatten has, I am aware, been taken to task for pointing out that the Punjab tragedy in terms of the Indian subcontinent involved only 3 per cent of the population. It has been stressed that this 3 per cent involved 90 per cent of the Sikhs and that in the total body politic the Punjab was in effect the heart.

On the assumption that a local Sikh-Muslim League settlement could alone provide the basic conditions of peace there, it has to be confessed that the provincial leaders of these two communities seem to have had as little inkling of their problem as of its solution. They were small men called upon to grapple with large events. They were in addition the victims of their own propaganda. The local Muslim League leaders claim to take over power in the Punjab with a 7 per cent communal majority was no more constructive than Sikh insistence upon the partition of the province and at the same time the retention of the right to choose which section of it they would join. There is no need to pursue this point further. There was no prevailing awareness of realities.

In face of such intransigence however, would it not have been an obvious precaution to have taken early steps to organize a wholesale transfer of populations? While the Sikh leaders might have been ready to have considered it, neither the Congress nor Muslim League High Commands would, so far as I am aware, countenance the project or hear of planning being made on such an assumption. The bitter truth is that only the compulsion of the communal mass killings and the fear of reprisals could have brought about the mass migrations. Economically such an exodus seemed to run wholly counter to the interests of the two new governments and the Congress and Muslim League must not be blamed for being averse to putting it into effect in advance of the event.

There has been criticism that in the light of their declared intentions we failed to take effective actions to suppress a Sikh uprising. Here again propaganda has outrun the available evidence. The civil administration was rapidly running down and as part of this process the intelligence service was under-staffed and over-strained. What evidence there was tended to show that in the Punjab there were plans involving violence emanating from all three communities but that the plans—such as they were—were based principally on local 'homemade activity'. A policy of suppression based on such an analysis would have been effective only by simultaneous action against all three communties. Such a policy would have placed an intolerable strain upon the communal loyalties of the strong forces needed to implement it. The forces were not available and the action would in any case have once again imperilled the wider political agreement. I was present in India both during the Bengal famine and the Punjab crisis. By any assessment whether of statistics or the scale of suffering I am convinced that the Bengal famine was by far the greater catastrophe. I say this only because the idea seems to have gained currency that what happened in the Punjab was a disaster on a wholly unprecedented scale. Unhappily it was very far from being so. The total casualty roll in the Punjab will never be precisely known but it was probably some 10 per cent of the estimated annual death rate from malaria in the subcontinent.

The Gains of Transfer

In addition to the administrative considerations, the early transfer of power had, I believe, the following advantages: duly recognized at the time. First, it provided the psychological impetus for the establishment of long term goodwill between Britain and the successor governments. Secondly, it enabled Dominion status to be tried out with the full agreement both of Congress and the Muslim League on a transitional and, if successful, on a permanent basis, and within this framework provided the greatest administrative reinforcement of all—continuity through the great Government of India Act of 1935.

Undoubtedly at the time Lord Mountbatten's most pressing problem was to hold together the semblance of an interim government. From the moment agreement was reached in June the centrifugal forces were of such overwhelming potency that they called forth all the Viceroy's powers of conciliation to hold the unitary regime together even until August.

Consolidating the Settlement

Up to 15 August it was generally conceded that the Viceroy had held the balance of power with reasonable fairness between the mighty opposites. I recall in particular the sentiments expressed both by Mr Jinnah in Karachi on 13 August and by Mr Nehru two days later at the Independence Day banquet at Government House, New Delhi. In accepting the Governor-Generalship of the Dominion of India Lord Mountbatten was *ipso facto* exposed to the criticism of having sacrificed his arbitral status. I am on record, however, as being one of those who firmly believed that this was an acceptable risk, that because Mr Jinnah, no doubt for compelling reasons of State, had decided to reject the concept of a joint Governor-Generalship, this in itself should not be the decisive reason for Lord Mountbatten refusing the unconditional offer of the Congress Party to remain on in the Indian Dominion.

I am firmly persuaded that when all the historical evidence is available this appreciation will be vindicated, and in spite of current propaganda, largely ill-formed, and even on occasion malicious, it will be shown that Lord Mountbatten, far from being anti-Muslim, was wholly dedicated to the task of consolidating the settlement he had done so much to produce. In his efforts to promote the stability and uphold the legitimate interests of Pakistan, it will be shown that he used all his influence throughout as a peace-maker mitigating differences between the two new governments and urging at all available opportunities moderation and restraint. It was in contrast with his Viceregal record, essentially an unspectacular backroom role, but it was appreciated at official levels both in Karachi and New Delhi. An example of this mutual confidence is the fact that at the request of and on behalf of both countries he continued to serve for the rest of his time in India as Chairman of the vital Joint Defence Council. Moreover as the Governor-General of the Dominion of India he was a head of a State with over 40 million Muslims within its borders.

Lord Mountbatten undoubtedly had differences of

opinion with Mr Jinnah as he had on occasion with the other leaders but these were nothing so profound as the daily strains and stresses might suggest. Mr Jinnah's coldness and austerity and his attitude to leadership were such as to preclude the usual gives and takes of human relationships or personal diplomacy. A man of more cordial temperament and less rigid belief in the maintenance of the single objective might well have weakened in his high resolve to create a Muslim homeland within the Indian subcontinent. Lord Mountbatten did not conceal his preference for a unitary solution even in his broadcast on 3 June, but at the same time he did not flinch from the logic of partition. In spite of the masochistic theme that Pakistan was crippled from birth the 3 June Plan laid the foundations of an economically viable and politically resilient State which has already established itself as one of the most stable in Asia.

Passing of the Princely Territories

As if the communal contentions were not enough there was superimposed the no less perplexing and dangerous problem of the Indian States. Here again there has been a large volume of misgiving over the policy adopted and its outcome and such terms as breach of faith and betrayal have been freely used. Once again I ask myself whether with the conditions confronting us at the time it would have been possible for Lord Mountbatten to have offered any advice other than to recommend accession. To have given no advice at all would merely have intensified the Princes' indecisions and uncertainties and opened up endless opportunities for intrigue. To have advised the Princes to stand out would, surely, in the context of our declared intention to transfer power to British India, have been a wrecking act of almost Trotskyite proportions for all concerned. To transfer power to two sovereign States covering two-thirds of the subcontinent and to leave a power vacuum in the remaining third would, in my judgement, have been morally far more questionable and politically more explosive than to pursue the course in fact adopted.

As I understand it the essence of treaties of paramountcy was the establishment of a relationship with the paramount power which involved for the Indian Princes a status less than that of either independence or full national sovereignty. The purpose of these treaties was presumably to stabilize the power of the Raj within the limits of its resources. On what principle of political equity could successor governments in British India, comprising citizens of the same kith and kin as those in the Indian States, be expected to guarantee the full independence which Paramountcy was designed to limit? And in the absence of such a guarantee what was such independence worth? Whereas there might have been margin for manoeuvre and compromise under a unitary dispensation, such as the Cabinet Mission Plan which provided for a weak centre, the logic of partition involved the substitution of two strong central authorities who neither politically nor administratively could afford to delegate their sovereignty any further.

It is against this context that the special case of Hyderabad for instance should be viewed. Indeed, the

three special cases of Hyderabad, Kashmir and Junagadh
are a warning of the immeasurable chaos that would
have ensued if the accession policy had not prevailed in
the remaining 570 States large and small. All that could
be done was done to persuade the Maharaja of Kashmir
and the Nizam of Hyderabad to accede in time. As far
as Kashmir was concerned, this was 15 August, on
which date I am convinced that his accession to either
power would have been accepted by the other. As for
Hyderabad the urgency lay in a dangerous upsurge of
communal passion in the heart of southern India which
had hitherto been immune from the infection.

Partition due to Communal Strife

It is this tremendous factor of communal politics which
invested the whole transfer of power with such a strange
sense of melodrama. I have said in my book that partition did not cause the communal crisis, but the communal crisis, partition. The interaction of rival Muslim
and Hindu nationalisms created an atmosphere of
frustrated revolution. There was a ready, almost too
ready, acceptance of deadlock on all sides. While the
leaders sat facing each other in this mood they themselves
were helping to establish a roadblock against their free-
dom. The technique of resistance undoubtedly created
complex tensions within Muslim and Hindu societies
which threatened to overwhelm the resources of
orthodox constitutional leadership and to trample under
foot the imported seeds of Western liberal democracy.
The Muslim League's Direct Action decision in August
1946 was to touch off an orgy killing and counter-

killing, but the causes of the massacre must surely reach out far beyond any one particular act of defiance.

I have read, of course, accounts of the origin and development of the Hindu, Muslim and Sikh conflict in which considerable emphasis has often been laid on economic and social as well as the purely religious factors, but when the hour of decision came what impressed me was the comparatively low priority accorded by leaders and people alike to economic self-interest or social solidarity. The economic interpreters of history; the dialectical materialists, readers of the gospel according to Karl Marx, all these determinists were swept away like chaff in the wind before the emotional hurricane induced by partition. As an example the Communists, who had picked the industrial slums of Calcutta and the overcrowded, undernourished province of Bengal as their centre of agitation, saw fit to nail their flag to an anti-partition policy which must have seemed to them to have highly exploitable possibilities, particularly in view of the strong Bengali nationalist sentiment. But when the Congress and Muslim League High Commands accepted the partition formula for the province the Communist campaign died away overnight. As a result they substantially switched their attention to more promising fields of operation in Hyderabad and Madras.

The Inevitable Army Divisions

But not only was there subordination of the economic and ideological to communal considerations, the pattern of military strategy had similarly to be fitted into the

27

demands of partition. Once again complaints that our terms for transferring power should have been the unity of the Indian Army or the postponement of its reconstitution ignore the prime elements of the situation with which Lord Mountbatten was called upon to deal. Such insistence would have smashed any partition plan from the outset. The immediate control of their own national armies was for the leaders on both sides the *sine qua non* of national independence—the symbols and touchstones of our good intentions. For it was after all a transfer of power not just some of the power with some still reserved for the British Government.

In view of its communal emphasis it is legitimate to ask what have been the strategic and economic consequences of partition? It is beyond the scope of this lecture to try and assess the answer, and the attempt would in any case probably be premature; none the less I would submit that there is already ample evidence to show that the more dire predictions of economic collapse and military impotence have not been fulfilled. Continuity has bred confidence, and confidence is breeding strength for India and Pakistan. The latest manifestation of this is the Indian general elections which in their conduct and result have exceeded the most optimistic forecast. They are a tonic to the democratic way of life everywhere. As for the role of those who have the primary responsibility for the form taken by the transfer of power, the dictum of Mr D W Brogan in his recent book *The Price of Revolution* should in all fairness be applied. For he wrote, 'It is an unwise statesman who spends too much time contemplating incalculable possibilities that he can neither foresee nor control.'

Multi-Nationalism

When the time came for the Western powers with colonial empires in the East to give effect to their declared intentions to hand over government, they were to find that the force and form of the racial and religious upsurge in Asia was different after the collapse of Japan from what they had anticipated. They were dealing not simply with nationalism but with multi-nationalism. The impact of the Japanese conquest and occupation had not only undermined the prestige of the Western powers among the indigenous peoples but also done much to destroy the unitary systems which they had so labouriously built up. It was the same story in nearly every country, Indonesia, Malaya, French Indo-China, Burma, as well as India itself. Nationalism then in finding its own level cut across the best laid plans that had been made for it by Western democracies. I believe that if the independence movements in these countries had been further frustrated this demand for smaller self-determination would have become even more clamant and effective than it is today, and it may well be that we have not seen the end of fragmentation in the area as a whole. As far as the Indian situation is concerned this process has been effectively halted, but only just in time.

It is sometimes asserted that the British governed in India on the principle of divide and rule and by such acts as the establishment of communal electorates with weightage under 1909 reforms were in fact in themselves the principal vivisectors. It is not for me to enter into speculation on such a subject before such an audience,

29

but my own belief is that the whole history of the British Raj was one of an effort, conscious or unconscious, to achieve unification and that such concessions as those contained in the Morley-Minto Reforms were no more than admissions that the forces ranged against the unification of the subcontinent were such that they could not be totally ignored. Independence through partition was not the culmination of the long-cherished aim, but it was none the less the response to a challenge as real as it was to many surprising.

Grat Achievements of Partition

It is not sufficient to say that if only the requisite statesmanship had been forthcoming unity could certainly have been preserved. A wealth of British genius and eminence, talent and service had been thrown into the task of its nourishment. The conflict that had preceded Hastings has not been liquidated with the departure of Mountbatten, but a *modus vivendi* was achieved based upon equity, compromise, acceptance, if not agreement, after discussion. It is in the controversies it has settled rather than in those it has aroused that I believe the historical significance of the transfer of power will lie. This settlement should be seen, not only in the life line of restraint and goodwill held out even during the darkest hours of crisis between India and Pakistan, but also in the evergrowing volume of friendship and understanding between Britain and the two new governments. The British Commonwealth has been transformed, not weakened. Its political theory has been enlarged. It is no sleight of hand which has enabled a Republic to take its place within and alongside a Monarchical concourse of peoples. But beyond even its impact upon the Commonwealth this settlement and the form it has taken is a world event of the first magnitude.

Cutting across pretensions of the free world, sapping the strength of the whole democratic cause has been a tragic discrepancy between theory and practice in racial relations, a widening gulf between the aspirations of East and West. It is my belief that the voluntary transfer of power to India and Pakistan has in its scope and breadth of vision reversed two of the most dangerous trends in the history of the modern world. By bringing such a vast proportion of the white and coloured races together on terms of an equality, unforced because mutually desired, it points the way to an integration of peoples which no amount of planning from above could achieve on its own.

The movements of mass opinion are still largely phenomena wrapped in mystery. The extraordinary revolution in sentiment that undoubtedly occurred in August 1947 was not just a single overwhelming demonstration of popular joy and goodwill. An enduring reconciliation has been too strong for propaganda to create or destroy. For those of us wholly absorbed in the final phase it was easy to overlook that there lay behind it two centuries of traditions of honour and trust which, when the time came to go, engendered neither bitterness nor taunts but generous thoughts and warm emotions. Perhaps I can best express this sense of historical synthesis by reference to a remarkable letter I read the other day from Dr Arthur Bryant to Lord Mountbatten, from which I am privileged to quote. His words may well be a prevision of posterity's considered verdict:

One day a Thucydides will write, I hope, the story of British India, and Nicholson at the Delhi Gate, the unsung district magistrate coping with plague, flood and famine in the course of duty, and your sudden transformation of the closing scene will all appear as facets of the same greatness.

Lord Listowel's Conclusion

Lord Listowel said that it would be agreed that the lecture had been fascinatingly interesting, and beautifully expressed. He would like to make three comments. The first was that he agreed with him that it was a profound misunderstanding to imagine that Lord Mountbatten was anti-Muslim. Lord Mountbatten accepted the post of Governor-General of India with utmost reluctance when he was asked to do so by Pandit Nehru. He consulted the Government of the day and the leaders of the Opposition and all were unanimous that he should accept the post, because it was realized that in spite of the difficulties which he would face and which he foresaw the alternative would have been far worse both for India and Pakistan. The alternative clearly would have been a Hindu as the first Governor-General of India, and, admirable as the Governors-General were after Lord Mountbatten, it was obvious that the friction between the two Dominions would have been even greater had they started without someone who had a great deal of Muslim goodwill and who did his best to act as a mediator between communal opinion.

The second point was with regard to the states. He profoundly agreed with the lecturer that the integration of the states in the Indian Dominions was a really remarkable step forward. He remembered when he first went to the India Office he was told by one of his mentors that it was the object of the British Government that the states should either amalgamate or join the provinces. That these small units should be merged seemed so advantageous from the administrative point of view, and from the point of view of social and political progress, that he accepted it as platitude. Endeavours had been made to do so for many years with little success, but it had now been achieved by the Indian Union. All the small states had been integrated into the Dominion in a very short span, to the advantage of the ordinary people who lived in these states.

The third point was the lecturer's reference to the importance of the inclusion of India as a republic to the whole concept of the Commonwealth. That was really a revolutionary step forward in the evolution of the British Commonwealth, almost as important as the Statute of Westminster. He remembered what a big problem this was. It should not be forgotten that it was decided at a conference of Prime Ministers by unanimous agreement that India should remain a member of the Commonwealth as a republic. Before that the Prime Minister had sent emissaries to every Dominion to explain to them the arguments in mind relating to the advantages and disadvantages. It was felt, on the whole, that the balance was a balance of advantage in accepting the severance of the Crown connection. He himself saw the Prime Ministers of Australia and New Zealand. The importance of the change was that it made the constitution of the Commonwealth more elastic, more fluid, and therefore more readily adaptable in the face of political change. India was not the only member of the Commonwealth which included people who entertained republican ideas, and it was the response of the Commonwealth to the changing political ideas of its members which enabled it to maintain its cohesion despite internal administrative and political changes.

Supreme Command
Earl Mountbatten of Burma

I CONFESS TO having awaited the publication of Philip Ziegler's official biography of Mountbatten* with high expectation, and just a trace of anxiety. Having served for six years on Mountbatten's staff and spent a further six compiling source material for just such a book, I considered the project sufficiently difficult to put at risk the historical reputation of subject and author alike. At the end of the fascinating 700-page journey, I can report confidently that Mountbatten passes the Ziegler test and Ziegler has met the Mountbatten challenge. The outcome is a biographical *tour de force*.

Towards the end of Mountbatten's life there was perhaps a danger of the story becoming trivialised and distorted; indeed, some of Mountbatten's latter-day involvement in pop projections of himself left Ziegler 'undeceived' but enraged to the point of momentarily losing his cool and complaining of his hero's 'determination to hoodwink him'. I doubt whether Mountbatten deceived anybody but himself with these exercises. Certainly during his mid-career, when I saw him on almost a daily basis, his vanity or egoism was more lighthearted than many critics—acquainted with him only as a septuagenarian on TV, or writing his own obituary—have taken to be the case. This was the period when he was successively Chief of Combined

* Philip Ziegler, *Mountbatten*, Collins, London.

Operations, Supreme Allied Commander, and Viceroy; and the scale, pace and level of his activities obliged him to lose himself in the demands of the job.

Just how dominant these were is brought out in the balance of Ziegler's narrative. Half the book is needed to cover those six momentous years, and to keep the story down to one volume the 'triple assignment' is if anything foreshortened. It is difficult to avoid the conclusion that had this 'interruption' to his naval career not occurred, and had Churchill not suddenly and dramatically extracted him from taking over command of the aircraft carrier *Illustrious*, Mountbatten would have been little more than a footnote to history. It is even doubtful whether an uninterrupted naval career would have led quite so inevitably to the fulfilment of his ultimate professional ambition of sitting in his father's chair as First Sea Lord.

Was Mountbatten's ambition as 'unbridled' as Ziegler asserts and some reviewers of the book assume? A conflict is indeed discernible here, best summed up in the proposition that inside every great man is a small man trying to get on. Once seconded to these high and special duties, Mountbatten's performance was in effect the reverse of ambitious. The terms of reference in each instance provided no precedents, only numerous danger signs and 'no-go' areas, the built-in resistance, national and international, of powerful military and political establishments. In dealing with this permanent high-risk situation, Mountbatten seemed to me to put the normal manifestations of ambition into cold storage and to act with almost arrogant indifference to his personal position.

Ziegler's densely packed narrative has not unnaturally inspired a wide range of reactions from a most distinguished posse of biographers. The assessments of Mountbatten spread across a spectrum from the 'genius' of Disraeli's Lord Blake to the 'lightweight' of Montogomery's Nigel Hamilton, with Asquith's Roy Jenkins plumping for 'a great "personality"' rather than a great man and Queen Victoria's Lady Longford going nap on 'his charm'. The life story of the Earl Mountbatten of Burma has provided rich critical pastures from the true-blue Toryism of Julian Amery to the up-market gossip of Alastair Forbes, from which Mountbatten emerges as

a man so various that he seemed to be
not one but all mankind's epitome.

In the welter of conflicting comment, discerning and sharp though much of it is, the impression remains that the full measure of Mountbatten has still to be taken.

There is no serious argument that, from the moment Queen Victoria took him in her arms at his christening, he was born great. Nor, from the moment Winston Churchill summoned him to Combined Operations with a blank cheque to act offensively and make it into a war-winning instrument, can it be gainsaid that he had greatness thrust upon him. Shakespeare's third test—whether thereafter he achieved greatness—I can best approach by delving into my experiences while I was on his staff and observing at increasingly close range his policy-making activities. But how great in conception, intrinsic status and formative historical influence were the three posts he was asked to fill? Ziegler, in persuit of the momentum of his hero's life story, provides only background evidence to this theme, and is not unnaturally more concerned with the player than the play. Some commentators in assessing Mountbatten's response have failed to do justice to the scale and immediacy of the challenge.

When, a month after the fall of France, Winston Churchill—'his mind working like the revolving beam of a lighthouse'—appointed Roger Keyes Director of Combined Operations, he was creating a revolution in the higher direction of the War which he duly consolidated fifteen months later when he replaced the senior and inflexible Keyes with the junior and amenable Mountbatten. As Bernard Fergusson in his classic history of Combined Operations, *The Watery Maze* (1961), succinctly put it: 'COHQ became not only the forcing house for new techniques and amphibious equipment; it became also the power-house for harnessing our maritime potential.' On Mountbatten's role he was similarly robust: 'There are still a few to decry the magnitude of Mountbatten's achievement; but historically speaking, to use a nautical phrase, they are spitting to windward.'

I arrived at Mountbatten's Combined Operations Headquarters two months before the ill-fated Dieppe Raid, having been posted there or rather 'invited to join the party' following a lively interrogation by the Chief of Combined Operations, who stressed that he wanted volunteers whose heart would be in the party's objectives. The place he wanted me to fill was that of Air Public Relations Officer, completing a group that already had representatives from the British and US Armies and the

Royal Marines, as well as a Commanding Officer from the RAF. But Mountbatten immediately qualified the word 'representatives': if I was to have any chance of success in the job I must forget the uniform I was wearing. He advised me that he took a direct and personal interest in public relations, which for him was not just a matter of devising publicity but a part of responsibility of command at the highest level. From then on, I was to be ever more closely involved with Mountbatten as communicator.

One of my marginal duties was to monitor enemy reactions on radio in the course of the Dieppe Raid. It became surprisingly clear to me that discordant notes were being struck in the enemy's jubilant propaganda, that political and military aims were confused during the first 48 hours and no serious efforts afterwards were made to reconcile them. In spite of all his other preoccupations, this point at once interested Mountbatten sufficiently to pass it on immediately to Brendan Bracken, the Minister of Information, confirming thereby the high priority he always gave to propagandist issues.

Post-mortems on the Dieppe Raid have tended to cast distorting shadows over Mountbatten's record and purpose as CCO. Its ambiguous origins and dubious command structure all point to failure arising from the application of too few rather than too many Combined Operations techniques and principles. This was borne in on me when I was assigned to the task of drafting the story of the highly successful St Nazaire Raid for what was to be a best-selling Ministry of Information booklet on Combined Operations. Ziegler covers that heroic enterprise a little too lightly—its planning and execution were in significant contrast to Dieppe. As Mountbatten wrote:

Of all the operations with which I was concerned in the late war . . . St Nazaire is perhaps the one I am most proud to have been associated with. . . . I know of no other case in naval or military annals of such effective damage being inflicted so swiftly with such economy of force.

After Dieppe the one-off raiding phase was superseded by Combined Operations' significant contributions to invasions in the Mediterranean theatre. The lessons from Dieppe also reinforced Mountbatten's case for the ultimate landing to be in Normandy, carrying (with his prize project, *Mulberry*) its own artificial harbour.

With Mountbatten's translation to the post of Supreme Allied Commander South-East Asia, the problem of his authority, the status of his assignment and the timing of his actions entered a new dimension. Once again Churchill's initiative had led to his appointment. Mountbatten continued to fit in to the Roosevelt-Churchill-Combined Chiefs of Staff system with its inter-allied and inter-service superstructure directing basically national and separate land, sea, and air forces. The only trouble was that within two months of Mountbatten pitching his camp in Delhi, the overt and effective *raison d'etre* of the Command had been removed from him. His appointment coincided with the acceptance, at the Quadrant conference, of a Pacific strategy which confined South-East Asia Command to little more than a holding role. Even within that framework, resources for independent amphibious operations were taken away from him. By January 1944 the cupboard was indeed bare.

At the age of forty-four Naval Captain, Acting Admiral, surrounded by a cadre of officers all far senior to himself but technically under his command, with Auchinleck relegated to commanding GHQ India as a supply base and Field Marshal Lord Wavell as Viceroy, he seemed, to put it mildly, vulnerable. My job as Recorder and War Diarist was to attend the big meetings and ensure that they were duly docketed in duplicate for London and Washington on instructions handed down from the President and the Prime Minister. I recall one particularly significant meeting on 31 January 1944 with Mountbatten and all his Commanders in Chief, together with his acidulated Deputy Supreme Commander, General Stilwell. Mountbatten was calling for support for the Axiom Mission led by the American General Wedemeyer, Mountbatten's Deputy Chief of Staff, to present a new strategy for SEAC in London and Washington. It was a tense, confused and complex encounter. Admiral Somerville (so senior that it embarrassd Mountbatten to take a salute from him) for much of the time reserved his position; Stilwell was at odds with everyone in general and with Wedemeyer in particular; yet somehow Mountbatten emerged with an authority over all that gold braid which he was never to lose.

I cannot extract from the notes precisely how this dominance was achieved, and no official record was made, but Mountbatten succeeded in implying at the outset that he had been placed in a position he had never sought, and if at the highest level there was any indication that he was not *persona grata*, he would not hesitate to go back to the President and the Prime Minister who had sent him there. If he had to do so, he would not like to answer for the consequences for those he left behind in high command.

That test over, he quickly settled an important difference with Auchinleck over reinforcing the Bengal-Assam Railway with American logistical assistance. At a private meeting I had with him on 19 February 1944, all his buoyancy had returned. My note records:

He spoke of the importance of the Axiom Mission . . . for the first time and outlying theatre of operations was exercising direct influence on world strategy . . . the present Arakan battle [the Battle of the Box] was 'one of the historic battles of the war'. Japanese troops were carrying out the same outflanking operation as last year, but now on a much larger scale. Where-as last year the enemy just outflanked us and we had to turn tail, now the same troops were standing firm. Nobody moved. This was a tremendous test. If we won this particular battle it would have the utmost morale consequence. . . .

As for the Chiefs of Staff [with whom he had to deal for resources], his policy towards them was to go ahead first and ask permission afterwards, which had the effect of putting the onus on them for the cancellation of specific operations. This was not always possible. But to wait upon their general approval was often to risk doing nothing at all.

The 'Battle of the Box' was duly won but less than a month later larger events had taken command of plans and blueprints. My private interview note for 23 March read:

Supreme Commander raised the question of the threat to Imphal—the decisions and action taken which he considered should be regarded as of historical importance. He said that although this threat had for some time been apparent there was an atmosphere of complete complacency at the various headquarters nor any apparent awareness of an imminent crisis. He said that if the Fifth Division had been transfered [from Arakan] by road the move would have started about the beginning of April and would not have been completed until the 24th April. He found that there had been made no provision for another division or for a division from India which he wanted. They only awoke to the danger following his two hour's talk with Slim on the 13th March; after this they were fully alive to the situation and almost more alarmed than he was.

He discussed the matter with the Army on Tuesday 14th March, with the Air Force on Wednesday 15th March. On Friday 17th March approval for transport aircraft was received and Monday 20th March 123 Brigade with mules and jeeps was being flown in.

Mountbatten's role in supplying and sustaining resources for the defence of Imphal was a decisive contribution, but one which he felt he should not have had to make. In the general context of the campaign, credit must be given to the importance he placed on grappling with malaria and fighting on through the monsoon period, and his permanent emphasis on the flow of communications with the troops through both the written and the spoken word—the SEAC newspaper and Radio SEAS. His own soap-box appearances in the jungle were carefully planned improvisations. 'They call you the forgotten Army—you are not forgotten—they have never heard of you!' But with him about, his audience knew they soon would. This was theatre and public relations in the best sense of that much abused term.

After the move from Delhi to Kandy, far too much time was taken up in what were to prove abortive wranglings over plans which like a mirage rose up only to disappear; but all the time Japanese power was being sapped, and General Slim was consummating a brilliant offensive over impossible terrain, with Rangoon captured by separate assaults a few hours before the monsoon. Then came Mountbatten's sudden call to Potsdam.

I had returned home to contest the general election and he asked me over to his house, Broadlands, advising me cryptically of the horrific atomic fate awaiting Japan. He was having to send back messages about the likely impact on SEAC's future role, including calling off at the last moment the need to invade Malaya and assuming responsibility for the whole of Indonesia and he feared that his Chief of Staff General Browning would think he had taken leave of his senses. 'There will be quite a lot for your Records to absorb', he said.

There was indeed a credibility gap in what Mountbatten was called upon to undertake. His so-called 'post-Surrender tasks' involved him in a baptism by total immersion. I still find it hard to believe that one man could have taken on board so many disparate but desperate problems—crisis piling on crisis—at one

and the same time. The title of Supreme Allied Commander assumed a meaning beyond anything originally
intended for it. Political as well as military responsibility
for 126 million people, half a dozen emerging nations,
three returning empires, and hundreds of thousands of
Allied and enemy prisoners-of-war. If ever a man was
grappling in darkness with destiny, that man was
Mountbatten in South-East Asia from the autumn of
1945 to the spring of 1946.

Lord Blake's attribution of 'genius' certainly applies
to his performance during this bizarre period. I detected,
when all this pressure was on, Mountbatten's instinctive
sense of the nature of power and his no less instinctive
sense of timing in meeting its demands. His policies
and actions were based on an understanding of those
forces as 'neutral'; his flair was in his skill in applying
communications (public and private) to assuage their
harsher realities. When out of the blue he learned that
he was to be the last Viceroy, he was already an authority on the transfer of power, having assumed it at Combined Operations, and remitted it in South-East Asia.

On the other side of the coin was his sensitivity to
and defence of his own power. When I handed over the
United States copy of the SEAC Rcords to the Pentagon
in April 1946, I was summoned into the presence of
General Eisenhower, the then US Chief of Staff. He
used the occasion to launch into a general dissertation
on the appropriate status of Supreme Allied
Commanders, saying that he thought that he and
Mountbatten were the only two officers in World War
II who had had 'a full work-out' in the position.

Reporting on the interview, I wrote to Mountbatten:

He contrasted Foch's position with his own. How Foch was no more than a 'god-damned liaison officer', while he, Eisenhower, landed four Divisions at Antwerp only to take all their ammunition from them for special support operations. This was action of a type which would have led to Foch's instant dismissal, but still he considered that the full circle had not yet been run. He believed that experience would show that the powers of the Supreme Commander in every theatre needed further extension. He would like to see the Supreme Commander of one nationality in a position to dismiss an inefficient or subordinate General of another. . . . At the end of the interview he turned to me and paid a tremendous spontaneous tribute to you. 'Dickie', he said with great emphasis, 'in my view is one of the great Commanders of this war.'

My third assignment with Mountbatten, this time in a civilian capacity, had me emerging from a backroom to a frontline position as the first and only Press Attache to a Viceroy. The title didn't matter much; the function did. I kept an informal diary of those climactic fifteen months. It was published under the title *Mission with Mountbatten* some four years after the events it described, and absorbed thereafter as a primary source into the bloodstream of quite a lot of literature about Indian independence and the last Viceroy.

Its forthcoming republication 34 years later may perhaps release me from returning to its mood or relying on its evidence, but for those who will be reading Ziegler for their first inside view, I can say that he has worked his way through the various controversies with a well-constructed and balanced narrative. Once again I must stress Mountbatten's insight into power and timing. By June 1947, power in the subcontinent had run out. A few days before the 3 June Plan for the partition of the subcontinent was announced, Phillip Talbot, one of the most discerning and best informed foreign correspondents (he represented the *Chicago Daily News*) wrote a special foreign policy report entitled 'The Independece of India', analysing the prolonged prologue of violence. He concluded:

Already the administration of India is so far run down that as one Indian expressed it 'the only reason why we have not fallen into anarchy is that people have not yet realised we are already there'. . . . If for any reason the transfer of power is delayed or a successor government or governments do not appear promptly the chances of disruption will increase.

As C. Rajagopalachari (the Indian elder statesman who succeeded Mountbatten as Governor-General) so wisely said, 'If you had not transferred power when you did there would have been no power to transfer.' General Ismay, no less sensitive to the destructive forces at work, confirmed the need for rapid decision.

One central issue was Mountbatten's relations with Jinnah. (A comparison could perhaps be made between Jinnah and de Gaulle—men of inflexible will and single sovereign purpose, haughty, cold and distant, and operating from privileged weakness, they both had a veto in their pockets until the final crunch.) For Jinnah the crunch came on 2 June 1947 when he took himself and the Viceroy to the brink of disaster, only to recover and save them both with a silent nod when Mountbatten accepted the Partition Plan on his behalf in the presence of other Indian leaders.

Far different but at times hardly more predictable was Mountbatten's relationship with Nehru. I had the good fortune to be present for their historic first encounter in Singapore, when Mountbatten was in the midst of his post-Surrender tasks. It was an event which certainly would not have taken place if Mountbatten had not insisted upon it. I belonged to the small minority on his staff in favour, and because I had met Nehru before the War, I was asked by Mountbatten to prepare a brief biography of him, and to come in for coffee after the family dinner. Mountbatten did all the talking, I noted, and Nehru nearly all the thinking. Mountbatten covered Indonesian problems, Potsdam, Indian troops in Java, Malayan unrest, the lot—which Nehru did his best to absorb. There was a happy moment at the end, when Mountbatten at his most expansive declared about one of the crises: 'In short, everything I did, I tried to think of in the light of history, what it will look like in ten year's time.'

'Yes', said Nehru, his slight sad smile betraying no trace of irony, 'that helps us to escape the present.' History was soon to decree that there would be no such escape for either of them.

Key participant at this famous meeting was of course Lady Mountbatten who was nearly trampled on at a reception in honour of Nehru; at no small risk he had helped to rescue her. Her contribution to the post-Surrender and Indian story is already legendary.* Whether she was psychologically competing with Mountbatten, or whether they were emotionally distanced from each other is immaterial. Historically it is their public partenership that really mattered. They were inextricably linked, and the Mountbattens are for-ever in the plural, as at different levels and in different spheres are the Brownings, the Lunts or the Webbs. The challenge and the response were well matched, but Edwina was involved at the human and personal end of it and took therefore the greater physical strain, to the point of self-destruction. They were in themselves a combined operation, a supreme command, and in the best sense Excellencies.

I will close as I began—with Mountbatten as com-municator. Briefly, he was throughout, rather than a writing or literary man, a talking or (in the jargon) an audio-visual man, who came to his prime just ahead of the television revolution. Here he differs from Churchill who so closely influenced him in so many other ways. Men of Churchill's and Gandhi's generation believed far more in the sufficiency of the message delivered direct to the living audience or individual reader—Churchill

---

* To name the contingent of influential women at the sides of the Indian leaders during the transfer of power is to take an impressive roll-call—the stern Miss Jinnah, Nan Pandit and Indira Gandhi, the Begum Liaquat Ali Khan, Maniben Patel, Rajkumari Amrit Kaur and the redoubtable Sarojini Naidu. I doubt whether a more formidable feminine array has been *in situ* at a critical moment in world history to support or influence the action.

once called television 'a terrifying enlargement of human power', and Gandhi distrusted radio's secret publics, preferring to write letters in his own hand. Mountbatten tended to be suspicious of and to underestimate what was written; he wanted always to simplify, to popularise, and in particular to photograph. He was a believer in developing and using an image, but had passed his political and personal zenith before that term came to its full meaning.

In my entry for 5 June 1947 in *Mission with Mountbatten*, I included a personal impression prepared at the request of an American press correspondent. 'Mountbatten is essentially an extrovert character who does not relish silence or solitude but is at his very best in public', I wrote. And after setting out most of the pluses and minuses which Philip Ziegler has duly elaborated, I felt bound to conclude, as I still feel after forty years: 'All in all a rare and refreshing spirit, and whether on the quater-deck or in Viceroy's House a democratic leader of the first magnitude.'

The Triple Assignment
1942–48

A Recorder's Reflections

IT IS A PRIVILEGE I deeply value to be allowed to provide the opening contribution to this seminar held under the auspices of the Hartley Institute so early in its academic life. I address you not as a stranger but as an old friend whose links with the University of Southampton go back forty years to the launching of the Fawley Foundation Lecture, and includes such support and encouragement as I could provide for the formidable Mountbatten archives to be transferred on loan from Broadlands to residence in the Hartley Library which could do full justice to them for posterity. The further inclusion of the Palmerston and Shaftesbury papers from the same source, and subsequent addition of those covering the Duke of Wellington's whole career, has in the course of a very few years turned Southampton University's Hartley Library from a venture with exciting possibilities into one of the most important and authoritative sources for the political, military and social history of Britain in the nineteenth and twentieth centuries. The level, range and volume of the documents housed here vindicates that claim, and historians from all over the world can be expected to explore and raid the riches of this treasure house.

It is now possible to envisage from the Hartley

Institute a long sequence of seminars providing background commentary upon, and context for, the massive material housed here. It is timely that the Mountbatten papers should be given such early treatment. Indeed for this participant who, I believe, is the last surviving member of Mountbatten's staff at all three of the Headquarters of the Chief of Combined Operations, Supreme Commander South-East Asia and Viceroy of India—only just in time! Already we are approaching the last of the fiftieth anniversary celebrations, and there is an overdue need to refresh our memories with some glimpses at what history looked like when it was actually being made without the benefit—and I sometimes think the burden—of hindsight.

Does having survived this long cause me substantially to revise my perception of events which, both officially and unofficially, I described or placed on record at the time in my successive mutations from Air Public Relations Officer Combined Operations Headquarters, to Officer in Charge of Inter-Allied Records Headquarters Supreme Allied Commander South-East Asia, to Press Attache to the Viceroy of India? The answer must substantially be 'No'. The main modification or refinement which I will try this morning to develop, is that I now sense that all three of Mountbatten's appointments were essentially linked, and that I now see them as, more by accident than design, stemming out of each other, and as having a common and unifying element in their basic terms of reference. They were all appointments of urgency and crisis and of growing historical significance as the world moved from a war to a post-war scenario inevitably caught up in the problems and techniques of transferring power. Furthermore, it needs to be emphasized that a planned transference was, and remains, by no means an automatic or easy way of resolving issues of power which is to be regarded as a neutral force whether seized or lost, and, in the last analysis, not readily to be disposed of by process of discussion and debate or by constructive and controllable action in advance of the event.

When Mountbatten was first appointed by Winston Churchill to be Adviser, and then upgraded to become Chief of Combined Operations with a place on the British Chiefs of Staff Committee, he brought with him, as far as I am aware, no experience in handling power within a framework of specific techniques and innovations.

In considering Mountbatten's passage from orthodox Naval posts 'special duties' in Combined Operations, South-East Asia and India as essentially a single assignment in three stages, I do so in part because the duties involved led into and out of each other. In each case an unprecedented transfer of power was involved. The stakes were high and ever higher, and the time in which the response would meet the challenge was short and grew ever shorter: the downside risks were enormous. At the personal level what was needed was what Winston Churchill, with the instinct of genius, recognized in Mountbatten—a vigorous mind, hyperactive, optimistic and above all, an officer from the outset unacquainted with defeat and defence, whose war was only for winning. All three episodes have been heavily and separately documented and subjected to critical exposure extensive enough to house a small library. Readers familiar with Philip Ziegler's massive and majestic official biography of Mountbatten will recall that those brief six years take no less than 330 of its 700 pages, and 26 of its 52 chapters. Indeed, without these six momentous years he might have been expected to have provided little more than a footnote to the history of our time rather than becoming one who, in Ziegler's very last words, 'flashed brilliantly across the face of the twentieth century. The meteor is extinguished but its glow lingers on in the mind's eye'.

The *mise en scene* for this dramatic transformation began with the Dunkirk deliverance which, while it allowed for Britain's physical survival as a nation, marked our expulsion from the European mainland and our inability freely to return across the channel under cover from the Royal Navy's mastery of the high seas.

With the final collapse of France, Churchill had immediately grasped the full strategic implications. Directives began pouring out of 10 Downing Street urging highest priority to be given to the design and construction of suitable landing craft. The accumulation of landing craft and supporting weaponry on a hitherto unimaginable scale would condition the length and indeed the outcome of the war. From henceforth there would need to be a new or fourth dimension of command with appropriate officers from all three Services, specialists and experimenters in new techniques of warfare. A transfer of power would be involved, affecting some of the most entrenched prerogatives of the Armed Forces.

To embody and give dramatic impetus to this process,

Admiral of the Fleet Sir Roger Keyes was summoned to become Director of Combined Operations. He accepted with alacrity and reacted with gusto. Four years older than Churchill himself, and vastly senior to everyone else, he regarded himself as answerable only to Churchill in his capacity as Minister of Defence. He was originally lodged in the Admiralty, but it did not take him long, following some conflict with their Lordships, to march out with his loyal band, and, crossing the road, take possession of some vacant accommodation in Richmond Terrace.

Thus turbulently was Combined Operations Headquarters born. But for all Keyes' offensive spirit he was not able to enlarge its original remit which Bernard Fergusson in *The Watery Maze*—his memorable story of Combined Operations—defined as being 'primarily to initiate and execute raids, to interfere with German preparations for invasion and to symbolize defiance. . . .' 'However', he added, 'when Keyes sought to stretch the bounds of his dominion to include the actual direction of all expeditions overseas, even his own most loyal and affectionate supporters realized he was sailing on the wrong course and would have to go.' When Mountbatten, extracted by Churchill from taking command of an aircraft carrier following his dramatic forays with the destroyer *Kelly*, was the surprise choice to succeed him, Fergusson claims that

the Service Ministries tended to believe that COHQ's wings ad been effectively clipped. They had fought and routed and Admiral of the Fleet who was one of the Prime Minister's oldest cronies. They had little to fear from a youthful

Captain in the Royal Navy. At first neither he nor the task assigned to him were taken seriously.

Mountbatten's approach to the problems of power and its transference were from the other end of the spectrum. He had on his side, Fergusson asserts,

youth, intelligence, imagination, enterprise and energy. His mind had not been shaped by long years in ministry moulds and he had a flare not only for new ideas of his own but still more for seeking out men who could develop these and contribute others.

With Mountbatten's subsequent promotion from Adviser to Chief of Combined Operations, Keyes felt aggrieved that Churchill had given to his successor the status which he had refused to allow to himself—but this was not so. Mountbatten was not being authorized to supersede or overrule the Chiefs of Staff. He and his Command were being grafted on to them. Post-Pearl Harbour, with America's entry into the war partnership, their role was at once enlarged—they became, informally but effectively, Joint Chiefs of Staff. Within a month of his promotion a visit of inspection to Mountbatten's Richmond Terrace Headquarters by General Marshall led to the US Chiefs of Staff sending officers of their three Services to become part of Mountbatten's team. 'COHQ', in the words of Vice-Admiral Sir Ronald Brockman in his chapter on Mountbatten for the symposium *The War Lords*,

thus became the first integrated, inter-allied, inter-service headquarters in history and the pre-runner of all that followed in the war. American units were also attached to Combined Operations for amphibious training and the strength of the

Command rose to 50,000 officers and men of the three services.

Consequent upon this historic transfer of power, three formative events or developments need briefly to be recorded. First, just ten days after the Marshall visit, Mountbatten's planners and raiders brought off a brilliant coup at Saint Nazaire. Achieving a high degree of tactical surprise, they injected the *Campbelltown*, a former US Lend-Lease destroyer, into the precincts of the dockyard, turning it into a block ship and filling it with explosives, then blowing it up, thus denying to the enemy for the rest of the war the only port large enough to house their formidable battleship *Tirpitz*.

This was to be followed some five months later, however, by a spectacular failure, the raid, or so-called 'Reconnaissance in Force', on Dieppe. The ambiguities and controversies surrounding this tragic event are endless and have been recalled mostly, but not exclusively, to Mountbatten's and COHQ's detriment. They tranced the purpose of this review which is to note the raid's impact on the larger power scene. At a critical planning stage, when he should have been presiding over the proceedings, Mountbatten was whisked away by Churchill to confer with President Roosevelt, and if possible pre-empt the risk of American landing craft being diverted from Europe into higher priorities against Japan in the Pacific. Dieppe emerged as the only surviving symbol of the Allies' serious intention to open a Second Front, not now, alas, in 1942, but as soon as possible thereafter.

Disagreements on implementation concealed a far

deeper divergence over where the ultimate location for the return to Europe should be. The formation at the end of 1941 of a Combined Commanders' Committee served only to sharpen the controversy, with General Sir Bernard Paget and Air Marshal Sir Sholto Douglas solidly in favour of the Pas de Calais, and Mountbatten, at considerable risk to his credibility and prospects of survival, holding out for Normandy and the Cottentin Peninsular. It is, I think, of considerable significance that Mountbatten deliberately chose to do battle on this vital issue as a Combined Commander rather than relying on his membership of the Chiefs of Staff Committee to overrule them.

Even more impressive was his initiative in organizing and presiding over the special conference held aboard *HMS Warren* (an hotel and not a ship, by the way) at Largs in Scotland under the code name 'Rattle'. According to Fergusson, on whose account I rely,

so eminent and numerous was the rank and position of those attending it, that the ribald christened it the Field of the Cloth of Gold. . . . Among those in attendance were 20 assorted Generals, 11 Air Marshals and Air Commodores, eight Admirals, and Brigadiers galore.

Fifteen Americans were also there. In assessing the level and range of the decisions clearing away, as they did, so many doubts and misgivings, Fergusson concludes that

in many ways "Rattle" was the summit of COHQ's achievement. It was "Rattle" that the final lodgement area (Normandy) was approved to the full satisfaction to those who at that time looked like bearing the personal responsibility for the greatest operation ever carried out.

He added,

It was splendidly produced, and carefully stage-managed, but there was no feeling that a confidence trick was being put across. Seven important officers sat at the high table. In the Chair was Mountbatten, the youngest of them by eight years.

At 'Rattle', COHQ's prize 'strange device', the Mulberry Harbour, was at last taken on board for genuine implementation.

At one blow with the removal of the need for the real invasion to capture an established port in a built-up area, Dieppe, ironically and quite unintentionally, served to become a potent deception operation helping to provide a plausible cover for the bizarre developments of Mulberry and Pluto (Pipeline Under The Ocean), while encouraging the German High Command to disrupt the balance it had struck between the Atlantic Wall's Perimeter and depth defences and to reinforce the former in the wrong places. 'Rattle', also confirmed the alliance between Combined Operations and the embryonic headquarters of what was to become in due course General Eisenhower's Supreme Command. By the autumn of 1943, power had been effectively transferred to Combined Operations and then from it to an integrated Supreme Command capable of exploiting to the full its unique know-how.

So, when Mountbatten himself was selected by Churchill and endorsed by Roosevelt to take charge of another Supreme Command in South-East Asia, Combined Operations' controlling role as a result of

'Rattle' was already past its zenith. It would, however, be a mistake to suggest that all was sweetness and light; for, as Fergusson pungently observes,

COHQ was rooted in dislike and grew in an atmosphere of distrust. There were officers in high positions—though not in the highest—who never ceased throughout the war to resent and combat its special position. Such of their juniors as shared their prejudice looked on the denizens of COHQ as a coven of deluded druids.

The principal sources of disaffection were within both the Admiralty and the War office, and Mountbatten was particularly sensitive to the enmity being enlarged and defined by his acquisition, as a mere substantive Captain, of an unprecedented inter-service and inter-allied post carrying with it the treble acting rank of full Admiral, and doing a General out of his job in the process.

Parallels with the Combined Operations assignment were immediately apparent. Total defeat—this time, at the hands of the Japanese; marginal escape and survival—this time, through the jungles of Burma; the need once again for exclusively offensive action; the development of an amphibious strategy, and with it, of course, the ever-dominant requirement for landing craft. The final need was to get a move on and out of the Burma cul-de-sac. Mountbatten was once again heavily out-gunned by the rank and experience of his Service Commanders, and he had as Deputy Supreme Commander a particularly prickly colleague in General Stilwell, not so affectionately known as Vinegar Joe. Mountbatten brought out with him high hopes soon to be dashed and firm resolve soon to be tested. Within weeks after his installation as Supremo, the Americans reasserted their firm intention to give top priority to Pacific strategy for the ultimate conquest of Japan, relegating SEAC from the outset to the role of a strategic sideshow.

I have read accounts of how Mountbatten, criticized for having been over-indulgent in accumulating staff at Combined Operations Headquarters, then went overboard with a vast army of some seven thousand bodies in South-East Asia. This is not accordance with the facts. He inherited special links and large established units of 11 Army Group, Eastern Fleet and an Air Command. His own Supreme Command embodied an inter-service team of under 500. However, as Brockman justly observes, 'the problem of establishing the Command structure was daunting and his subordinate Commanders in Chief and his Deputy would need very careful handling'.

There was from the outset a political as well as a military dimension involved. Stilwell had in fact acquired no less than four different posts at four different levels, answerable in only one of them directly to Mountbatten as Supreme Commander—the others sharing his grudging allegiance, the US Government, the US Chiefs of Staff and Generalissimo Chiang Kai Shek. It was a scenario worthy of Alice in Wonderland and the Mad Hatter's Tea party.

Also at odds with the concept of a unifying Supreme Allied Commander was his operational relationship with Eastern Fleet. Here the Admiralty, while allowing the Naval Commander-in-Chief to be subordinate to the Supreme Commander in all matters concerning security and support of the land campaign and amphibious operations in the theatre, insisted on his remaining answerable to their Lordships for wider operations in regard to the security of sea communications and with offensive action at sea against the enemy. Mountbatten at the time of his appointment had protested in vain to the First Sea Lord (Dudley Pound) against this built-in ambiguity. Fortunately the goodwill of the successive Eastern Fleet Commanders, Admirals Fraser and Power, replaced the good sense that had been missing.

Equally ambivalent was the relationship with India Command as far as land forces were concerned. Here, bearing in mind how heavily dependent South-East Asia Command would be on Indian troops to sustain our operational capability in Burma and beyond, the British Government, in Brockman's words

decided it was constitutionally impracticable to place troops in India under a Commander not responsible to the Government of India. They further considered the two Commands were too large for one man to manage effectively. SEAC therefore retained control of operations and India became the base of all three Services, both Commands remaining equal.

It must, however, have been particularly galling for an officer of General Auchinleck's stature and battle experience to find his operational powers taken away from his grasp to be handed over to a Naval Captain acting Admiral, and it might well have been what Brockman called 'an unworkable proposition' but for Auchinleck's magnanimity and Mountbatten's tact engendering again the necessary goodwill.

It was, however, in the development of the Air Force within his Command that, to quote Brockman again,

it may unquestionably be said that Mountbatten made one of his greatest contributions to the success of the South-East Asia campaign. He was so dissatisfied with the separate control of British and US Air Forces that on 11 December 1943, he issued a directive of great political consequence. He turned the British Air Commander-in-Chief into the Allied Air Commander-in-Chief with all the air forces under him. He grouped the RAF and US Army Air Forces in Burma into a single integrated force under the US Air General (General Stratemeyer). Great improvement in morale and efficiency resulted.

This was indeed a crucial transfer of power, and it was made only just in time. The forcing-house in Burma was provided by the Japanese themselves, first in the Arakan and then on a far bigger scale in the Imphal area to the north, when they developed flanking attacks in the expectation of defending forces having to retreat back on their supply lines, but the order came now to stand firm and await supply, which duly arrived, from the air. This *coup de main* was only achieved by Mountbatten twice in close succession taking it upon himself to divert American transport aircraft from their regular supply missions to China over the Himalayan hump and, in the process, directly disobeying President Roosevelt's clear order not to do so the first time, and certainly not again. With the unauthorized backing of thirty US transport aircraft, two whole divisions were moved from the Arakan to the central front, there to lay the foundations for General Slim's and his 14th

Army's historic break-out and ultimate break-through, to Rangoon. The entire operation was rendered possible throughout only by Anglo-American air support of heroic proportions, and at high risk maintained at double the recommended sustained rate not just over a few days, but over months on end.

The same propensity for applying original priorities at Combined Operations now served to provide crucial backing for Slim's brilliant direction of the 14th Army and its reconquest of Burma. From the outset Mountbatten recognized the combined impact of malaria and the monsoon as being more deadly and debilitating than the fanatical Japanese themselves. By setting up a high-level specialist medical team with experts to tropical disease he was able to reduce the ratio of sickness to battle casualties from a crippling 120:1 to a feasible 10:1, thereby making good what had seemed to be at the outset a vain boast on his part to continue the campaign without interruption throughout the monsoon. Such initiatives are the true ingredients of victory in war. Slim in his greatness had no doubt. 'We did it together', he said.

But with the sudden collapse of Japan following upon the nuclear bombing of Hiroshima and Nagasaki, South-East Asia—a strategic sideshow in war—covering an area as large as Europe, encompassing a population of over 120 million, was suddenly caught up in a vast power vacuum liable to be filled up at any moment by violent and anarchic forces. Mountbatten, at Potsdam, found himself the recipient of huge new segment to his Command—the whole of Indonesia, no less. The complexities of transferring power were deepened and magnified beyond what any normal guidelines could be expected to quantify. Mountbatten's annexe to his Dispatches, entitled *Post-Surrender Tasks* (which was not authorized to be published for many years after the war), does its best to soften the impact of the drama which he was to confront. It became abundantly clear that four years of Japanese occupation was in itself a species of time-bomb, and created an environment which could not accept a simple restoration of pre-war power for all those high officials locked away in cold storage and waiting, as of right, to be set up again in the seats of Imperial authority from which they had been so rudely ejected.

In the welter of conflicting claims and obligations, Mountbatten moved his Command Headquarters from Kandy to Singapore to be somewhat nearer the centre of the action. Finding himself by a sudden transmutation in effect the Military Governor of the whole of South-East Asia, he was called upon simultaneously to cope with the power claims of Aung San and his Nationalist guerillas in Burma; with embryonic Communist agitation in Malaya and Singapore; with Indo-China arbitrarily partitioned at the 16th Parallel—French Gaullist versus Vichyite to the South of it, Chiang Kai Shek's bailiwick to the North, and with Ho Chi Minh lurking somewhere in the wings, in due course to supersede the lot; with Indonesia containing Suekarno firmly installed by a large undefeated Japanese Army, and the Dutch automatically expecting to be re-installed and to replace him; and with Thailand, technically an enemy defeated in a war which it had not been called upon to fight, but now summoned to sign a Peace Treaty, thereby releasing its rich rice granary to help stave off the threats of starvation throughout the whole area.

Superimposed on all this was the desperate problem of repatriating a vast army of Allied prisoners of war, in which process Lady Mountbatten, invested with Red Cross and St John's authority, herself earned fame and provided heroic support.

Everywhere the central problem was how to transfer sustainable power which extended his military remit farther than could ever have been envisaged into political arenas, and as such was a baptism by total immersion. Brockman who as his Naval Secretary was at his side from South-East Asia days onwards in all his various posts for twenty years, and was in a unique position to assess his Chief's overall performance, speaks of these accumulated post-surrender responsibilities bringing with them

daunting political and administrative problems. He faced and tackled them with his characteristic self-confidence, vigour and clarity of mind, supported by a wise liberal attitude which set a tone for future relations with the populations of Colonial territories.

I was privileged to be a colleague of Brockman and Mountbatten's staff both in South-East Asia and in India, and I wholeheartedly endorse his judgement. However, lacking the admirable professional reserve of the silent Service, my reactions went a little further. In a profile published in the magazine *Encounter* at the time of publication of Ziegler's official biography in 1985, I wrote,

If ever a man was grappling in darkness with destiny, that

was Mountbatten in South-East Asia from the autumn of 1945 to the spring 1946. Lord Blake's attribution of "genius" certainly applies to his performance during this frenetic period. I detected, when all this pressure was on, Mountbatten's instinctive sense of the nature of power, and his no less instinctive sense of timing to meet its demands. His flair was in his skill in applying communications (public and private) to assuage their harsher realities. When out of the blue he learned that he was to be the last Viceroy, he was already an authority on the transfer of power, having assumed it at Combined Operations and remitted it in South-East Asia.

So I reach belatedly, but not, I hope, irrelevantly, the climax of Mountbatten's involvement with transferring power—his appointment by the Prime Minister, Mr Attlee, and the Labour Government, after the briefest of vacations and return to Naval duties, to replace Lord Wavell, and to become the last Viceroy of India. While I do not expect many of you to have read the daily account of my experiences in the post of first and last Press Attache to a Viceroy, you will not expect me to take you through or analyse in details this historic transaction. It has been the subject of extensive critical study of widely varying range and quality over the years, and in any case you will shortly have the benefit of Professor Talbot addressing himself exclusively to the subject.

It will meet my purpose here if I concentrate on what I regard as the central issue of this Address—that by becoming Viceroy of India in 1947 he was returning, but on a larger and more momentous scale, to what was essentially the same assignment that he had been called upon to undertake at Combined Operations and South-East Asia. Towards the end of his life he was under constant pressure to provide enterprising authors and journalists with 'The Inside Story' of his real part in the attainment of India's and Pakistan's Independence. Equally he was at pains to retail his version of events on television within the twelve part documentary 'Mountbattens's Life and Times'. But the outcome has not, frankly, been entirely successful, has tended to induce rather more heat than light, and, at times, to trivialise and distort issues. In a long correspondence he had with me over the years, Mountbatten from time to time would ask if I could throw a little of the latter on some given point of contention.

This led me in a letter dated 6 October 1975 to react in some depth to a memorandum he was preparing—namely to answer the question, 'Was the speed of transfer responsible for massacres?' In it I submitted to him the following analysis which 21 years later I feel justified in incorporating into this Address, for it represents a perspective to which I still firmly adhere. I wrote as follows:

What I am still in doubt about is the form and emphasis of the question to which the memo addresses itself. To stay with the question as worded—"Was speed of transfer responsible for massacres?" distorts and narrows the perspective and puts you in a far more defensive posture than is either desirable or necessary. The question that in historical terms needs consideration—even though it is hypothetical—is what kind of a holocaust would we have been dealing with if there had been no political settlement and a mere demission to whomsoever might have seen fit to appoint themselves as our successors at the terminal date of June 30th 1948? Wavell's alternative solution upon which you needed to improve was a phased military withdrawl—no more no less. In the light of our experience the consequences of that do not bear thinking about.

My advice would be to continue to uphold the case for the speed of transfer within the framework of three sets of wise words attributable to Ismay, Rajagopalachari and Lloyd George, for they do help to put the issue in its full perspective.

1. Ismay's comment upon your becoming Viceroy was that it was "like taking command of a ship in mid-ocean with fire on the decks and ammunition in the hold". He said this to illustrate his thesis that India in March 1947 provided the most dangerous situation affecting the civil order that he had ever seen anywhere in peace time. Lawlessness, riots and bloodshed had, as your memo shows, already escalated to this point well in advance of our arrival on the scene. With political uncertainty and the run down of the civil authority the communal crisis had gained enough hold to constitute an immediate revolutionary threat to the entire subcontinent. I would quote here from your Viceroyalty Report for the period of 22 March–15 April. "By the end of my first week in office it had, indeed, become apparent that I would find the beginnings of an extensive civil war on my hands unless quick action were taken. It was becoming clear that an early decision was the only way of converting Indian minds from their present emotionalism to stark realism; and of countering the spread of strife, but at that stage there appeared to be little common ground on which to build any agreed solution for the future of India".

2. It was this sombre context which gave such force to the dictum of Rajagopalachari that "If you had not transferred power when you did here would have been no power to

transfer". It cannot be too strongly stressed that by March 1947 political negotiations had been going on virtually without a break and at the highest level for over two years. Although the various plans had proved abortive, the parties and personalities involved had come sufficiently near to success for great expectations to have been aroused and with failure for corresponding tension and frustration to have been induced. In this context June 1948 was indeed the end of the road; for any solution based upon the leaders' consent and readiness to compromise within that deadline was, by definition, to forestall the prospects of anarchy and to allow more time for successor Governments to stave it off. The scale and intensity of the Punjab tragedy has perhaps stood in the way of this point's being properly appreciated, but as you have rightly pointed out, 97 per cent of India's population was unaffected and enjoyed the maximum administrative continuity when the time came for us to go.

3. This leads me to recall Lloyd George's wise words that "You cannot leap across a precipice in two jumps." This precisely what those who wanted to delay and mitigate the process by putting administrative preconditions to the transfer of political power were trying to do. R.A. Butler is perhaps the most important exponent of this point of view. He aptly called his autobiography *The Art of the Possible*. He would, I am convinced, have been hard put to it to reconcile that principle with keeping the Interim Government in being a day longer than you did, and if you had not given top priority to a political settlement you would have been reduced to Section 93 rule within hours of taking over, and with due respect to Rab, that would have been practising the "Art of the Impossible".

In short, Mountbatten's Viceroyalty was the end of an end-game which had been conducted for not just two but five years by the same players familiar with every move and counter-move. All the principal personalities, men of high calibre, were lawyers skilled in the arts of special pleading; but within that framework they had indeed become 'senior citizens' whose experiences of actual power had been confined to agitation. Of all the leaders, the one who set the highest priority to changing his role of agitator and becoming an administrator, was Vallabhbhai Patel.

While Mountbatten was strictly an amateur when it came to political dialectic he revelled in verbal argument and debate, and by the time he reached Delhi he had become highly skilled at it. Recognition that time was running out was mutual on all sides. Once agreement was reached, Mountbatten did not rush events, events rushed Mountbatten. Immediately after the leaders had accepted the Partition formula, Mountbatten presented them with a paper entitled *The Administrative Consequences of Partition* which all concerned found no difficulty in handing down to three trusted subordinates, one of whom had actually written the document, and who in their turn found it relatively easy to clear up points of contention.

The role of the Interim Government, set up after the breakdown of the Cabinet Mission Plan, was at an end and it effectively disintegrated. The biggest danger throughout was the possibility that one or the other of the leaders would renege and relapse into the policy of negation and denial, from which veto all the parties would be the losers. Mountbatten was well aware of this traumatic risk and it conditioned his attitude to the problem throughout.

71

It was just such a context that led Woodrow Wyatt when reviewing my book *Mission With Mountbatten* 44 years ago, to reach a surprising but, I believe, valid conclusion. Wyatt as a young Labour MP had in 1946 been personal assistant to Sir Stafford Cripps in his capacity as member of the Cabinet Mission, the British Government's last abortive attempt to achieve united Indian independence, and was well placed to assess the key personalities, issues and motives involved.

Having paid tribute to Mountbatten's charm and energy without which he could never have persuaded Congress and Jinnah to accept what they largely disapproved of, Wyatt went on to say,

His only failure was Jinnah, who thawed less under Mountbatten's extrovert friendliness than anyone else and who was disliked by the Viceroy; but Mountbatten's dislike of Jinnah made him anxious to be fair to the Moslem League, so that on balance they gained slightly more than they would have done if Mountbatten and Jinnah had been as friendly as Mountbatten and Nehru.

When Jinnah, after allowing Mountbatten to believe that the temporary joint Indo-Pakistan Governor-Generalship might serve Pakistan's interest, finally rejected the idea and came down in favour of himself, Mountbatten had to face up to a real crisis. Lady Mountbatten, who well knew how far it was wise or appropriate to pressure her husband, urged him to leave and not stay on after 15 August on the grounds that he would have lost his impartial status. After much anxious soul-searching and double-checking, in which I myself was quite heavily involved, he finally accepted